W9-BUB-362

WHAT YOU NEED TO KNOW ABOUT
OBESITY

BY NANCY DICKMANN

CONSULTANT:
MARJORIE J. HOGAN, MD
UNIVERSITY OF MINNESOTA
AND HENNEPIN COUNTY MEDICAL CENTER
ASSOCIATE PROFESSOR OF PEDIATRICS
AND PEDIATRICIAN

CAPSTONE PRESS
a capstone imprint

Fact Finders Books are published by Capstone Press,
1710 Roe Crest Drive, North Mankato, Minnesota 56003
www.mycapstone.com

Library of Congress Cataloging-in-Publication Data
Library of Congress Cataloging-in-Publication Data
Names: Dickmann, Nancy, author.
Title: What you need to know about obesity / by Nancy Dickmann.
Other titles: Fact finders. Focus on health.
Description: North Mankato, Minnesota : Capstone Press, a Capstone imprint,
  [2017] | Series: Fact finders. Focus on health | Audience: Ages 8-11.? |
  Audience: Grades 4 to 6.? | Includes bibliographical references and index.
Identifiers: LCCN 2016000261|
ISBN 9781491482438 (library binding) |
ISBN 9781491482476 (paperback) |
ISBN 9781491482513 (eBook PDF)
Subjects: LCSH: Obesity—Juvenile literature.
Classification: LCC RC628 .D53 2017 | DDC 616.3/98—dc23

LC record available at http://lccn.loc.gov/2016000261

Produced by Brown Bear Books Ltd.
Editor: Tracey Kelly
Design Manager: Keith Davis
Editorial Director: Lindsey Lowe
Children's Publisher: Anne O'Daly
Picture Manager: Sophie Mortimer
Production Manager: Alastair Gourlay

Photo Credits
Front Cover: Shutterstock: (top); Science Photo Library: Power and Syred (bottom).
Inside: 1, © Thinkstock/Stockbyte. 3, © Shutterstock/A N Protatsov. 4 (bottom), © Shutterstock. 5, © Science Photo Library/ Dr Chris Hale. 6 (center), © FLPA/Albert Lleal/Minden Pictures. 6 (bottom right), © Science Photo Library/Stev Gschmeissner. 7, © Shutterstock: Vadim Bukharin. 8, © Science Photo Library/Eye of Science. 9 (top), © Shutterstock/A N Protatsov. 10, © Science Photo Library/Eye of Science. 11, © Science Photo Library/Eye of Science. 12, © Shutterstock/Samuel Borges Photography. 13, © HeadLiceGirlsBainbridge. 14, © Shutterstock. 15 (left), © Thinkstock/istockphoto. 15 (right), © Thinkstock/Jose Elias. 16, © Thinkstock/istockphoto. 17, © Shutterstock: Spotmatick Ltd. 18, © Shutterstock/Monkey Business images. 19, © Amazon. 21, © Thinkstock/Justin Cleary; 22, © Thinkstock/Mike Watson Images; 23, © Getty Images: Mediator Medical; 24, © Thinkstock/ Laura Cruise. 25 (top), © Thinkstock/istockphoto. 25 (center), © Shutterstock/Lopolo. 26, © Shutterstock: Sergey Novikov. 27, © Shutterstock: O M Oliver. 28, © Thinkstock/Stretch Photography. 29, © Dreamstime/Monkey Business Images.

Brown Bear Books has made every attempt to contact the copyright holder.
If anyone has any information please contact licensing@brownbearbooks.co.uk

007686WKTF16

Printed in China

TABLE OF CONTENTS

CHAPTER 1

WHAT IS OBESITY?

Our bodies are made up of many different things: bones, muscles, organs, and more. One important substance in your body is something called fat, or adipose tissue. It is made up of cells that store fat, and it is usually found under the skin. Your body can burn fat to release **energy**, so fat cells are a useful way of storing energy. This energy can be used if your body needs it later.

▲ Fat cells store energy for when the body needs it during exercise.

◀ When we eat more than our body needs, some of the extra energy gets stored as fat.

However, many people have too much **body fat**, and this can cause a variety of health problems. A person who is **overweight** is someone who has more body fat than is healthy. **Obesity** is a term used to describe someone who is very overweight. Doctors urge patients who are overweight or obese to change their eating and exercise habits. This is so that they can get down to a healthy weight.

energy—the ability to do work. Human beings get their energy from food.

body fat—tissue in the body that is made of up cells that store fat. It is also called adipose tissue.

overweight—weighing more than is healthy for a person's age, height, and build

obesity—the condition of being very overweight

BODY MASS INDEX

Depending on who you ask, definitions of being overweight or obese can be different. Many doctors use something called **body mass index** (BMI) to assess whether someone is obese. This is a simple mathematical formula that uses a person's height and weight. Most doctors agree that adults with a BMI between 18.5 and 25 are of normal weight. Those with a BMI between 25 and 30 are classed as overweight. People over 30 BMI are considered obese.

However, BMI isn't always accurate for everyone. For example, some professional athletes have BMIs that put them in the overweight category. They have very little body fat, but they have well-developed muscles. Muscle tissue weighs more than fat.

▶ Olympic shot-putter Valerie Adams has a BMI in the overweight range, even though she is fit and healthy.

BMI can be a useful tool. However, doctors have other ways of measuring body fat, such as physically measuring fat with a caliper. He or she may also take body measurements with a tape measure.

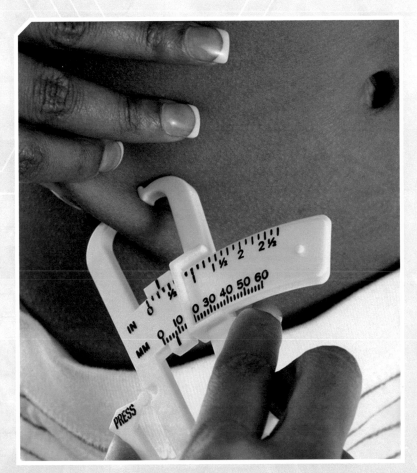

◀ Sometimes doctors measure the amount of body fat a person has with an instrument called a caliper.

body mass index—a formula that compares height to weight to estimate how much body fat a person has. It is often shortened to BMI.

BMI IN CHILDREN

Children grow at different rates at various times. Because of this, BMI numbers on their own are not always the best way to tell if a child is overweight. Instead, a child's BMI is compared to others of the same age. This is done using something called **percentiles**.

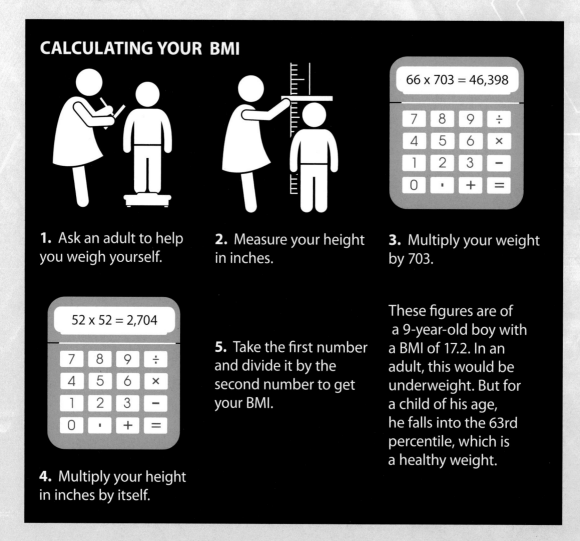

CALCULATING YOUR BMI

1. Ask an adult to help you weigh yourself.

2. Measure your height in inches.

3. Multiply your weight by 703.

66 x 703 = 46,398

52 x 52 = 2,704

4. Multiply your height in inches by itself.

5. Take the first number and divide it by the second number to get your BMI.

These figures are of a 9-year-old boy with a BMI of 17.2. In an adult, this would be underweight. But for a child of his age, he falls into the 63rd percentile, which is a healthy weight.

Scientists collect data about height and weight from millions of children. They use this data to make charts that show averages for each age. A percentile shows where one child's height or weight falls against the average. For a boy in the 70th height percentile, 70 percent of boys will be the same height or shorter. The other boys his age will be taller. Most pediatricians agree that a child with a BMI that falls between the 85th and 95th percentiles is overweight. A child whose BMI reaches the 95th percentile or above is considered obese.

▲ An early growth spurt can mean that one child might be a lot taller than another of the same age.

percentile—a value on a scale of 100 that shows the percentage that is equal to or below it

BMI AND ILLNESS

Keeping your weight under control can have benefits for your health. People who are overweight or obese have a higher risk of developing serious health problems. These include high blood pressure, high cholesterol, heart disease, arthritis, and some types of cancers.

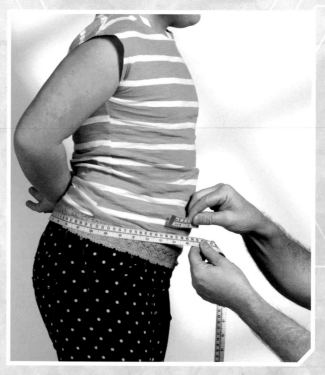

▲ Your doctor will tell you about the many health risks of being overweight. He or she will help you plan a healthier, more active lifestyle.

One of the most common conditions associated with obesity is Type 2 **diabetes**. This is a condition where too much sugar stays in a person's bloodstream. The symptoms of having high blood sugar are feeling thirsty and having to use the bathroom a lot. The person feels tired much of the time because his or her body can't use sugar effectively. Not enough energy is being made.

Taylor was only 12, but he weighed 250 pounds (113 kilograms). He had to take pills for Type 2 diabetes. He also couldn't run for long before his knees started to hurt, and he felt out of breath. Taylor's parents worked with him to swap fatty foods for healthier ones. They went on walks too, and soon Taylor began to lose weight.

▶ Some people with Type 2 diabetes must give themselves regular injections of artificial insulin. Insulin helps the body control sugar levels.

diabetes—a disease in which the body cannot control the amount of sugar in the blood

CHAPTER 2

WHAT CAUSES OBESITY?

To understand why some people are overweight or obese, you need to know what your body does with the food you eat. Most foods can be divided into three broad categories: **proteins**, **carbohydrates**, and **fats**. Proteins can be used as building blocks, to help your body grow new cells. Carbohydrates can be burned to produce energy. Fats are rich in energy, and they do many important jobs.

When you eat, your digestive system breaks food down into different nutrients.

Carbohydrates are turned into sugars and sent through the blood to all parts of the body to provide energy.

Any extra carbohydrates are stored as fat, or adipose tissue.

If you continue to eat more food than your body needs, fat will build to unhealthy levels.

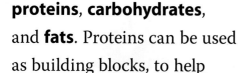

▲ If you eat a healthy diet and stay active, your body will burn up most of the energy from the food you eat.

After you eat, your body breaks the food down into its various parts so that it can be used. Carbohydrates are burned to provide energy for your body's cells. If you eat more carbohydrates than your body needs, any leftovers can be turned into fat for long-term storage. Extra fat is stored in the same way. If your body ever runs out of carbohydrates, it can burn these fat stores for energy. But if you always eat enough so that you never run short of energy, your body keeps storing more fat.

protein—a natural substance that the body uses to build and repair itself. Protein is found in all living things.

carbohydrate—a substance found in foods that provides energy for the body

fat—a substance found in foods that provides energy and does other important jobs in the body

OTHER CAUSES

Obesity is more complicated than simply eating too much. A person's lifestyle plays an important role too. Many people just aren't active enough to use up the energy in the food they eat. These days, many people spend hours in front of televisions, computers, or other gadgets. Cars have replaced walking as the main method of transportation for children and adults.

HEALTH FACT

Eating too much is not the only cause of obesity. Some rare genetic conditions can cause people to be overweight. Certain medicines can cause a person to gain weight as a side effect. Lack of sleep can also increase the risk of obesity.

◀ Playing games on your phone is fun, but it doesn't use up much energy.

Scientific studies have shown that obesity can run in families. If one or both of your parents are overweight or obese, then it is more likely that you will be too. Even identical twins brought up in different families often have a similar weight. This is so even if their diet and lifestyle have been very different. This shows that your **genes** have an effect on your weight.

▲ People who are related share many genes. Genes can affect everything from eye color to how your body uses food.

▶ If you don't get enough sleep, your body produces a chemical that makes you feel hungry. This is true even if you have eaten enough.

gene—a code in a body's cells that tells it how to grow. Genes control characteristics such as hair color.

MYTHS ABOUT OBESITY

There are a lot of myths and misunderstanding about obesity, especially when it affects children. Some people think that anyone who is overweight or obese is lazy. Some also assume that obese people don't have much willpower. But scientists have proven that unhealthy diets or inactive lifestyles are only one possible cause of obesity. One study even showed that obese children and adults in Canada were just as active as those of a healthy weight.

▲ Some children feel self-conscious about their weight and may be shy about joining in games with others.

ALLY'S STORY

The medication that Ally was taking made her gain 60 pounds (27 kg). Her classmates and even some friends began to tease and bully her about her weight. Her mother was able to help her deal with it though. Ally now helps other children who are going through the same thing, giving them advice when they're upset.

Many parents are reluctant to admit that their child has a weight problem. They might think that he or she will eventually grow into the extra weight. However, a child who is overweight is just as likely to continue to gain weight as he or she is to lose it.

▶ Children who are physically active have a better chance of staying at a healthy weight for life.

CHAPTER 3

TREATING OBESITY

If you think you may have a problem with your weight, see your doctor. He or she will weigh and measure you. Then the doctor will be able to tell if you have more body fat than is healthy. You will be asked a lot of questions about your lifestyle. This will allow your doctor to suggest changes that will help you get down to a healthy weight.

HEALTH FACT

The energy in food is measured in **calories**. Many foods are labeled as low-fat, but that doesn't necessarily mean that they are low in calories. Some of these foods have extra sugar added—sugar that your body will store as fat.

◀ Switching to a healthier diet gives you a good reason to try new foods. You may find something you really love!

◀ Read labels carefully to find out how many calories are in the foods you eat.

Changing your eating habits is often the first step to healthy weight loss. Swapping fatty or sugary foods for healthier options such as lean meat and vegetables is a good start. Eating smaller portions will help too. Your doctor can suggest foods that are filling without being fattening. Replacing soda and juice with water is another good idea.

▶ You don't have to give up all your favorite foods. Just limit them to occasional treats, and keep the portions small.

calorie—a unit used to measure the energy in food

EXERCISE

Becoming more active is just as important as cutting down on what you eat. When you are physically active, your body burns the calories in your food. If you burn more calories than you take in, your body will start to burn the fat that it has stored. You will then lose weight.

HEALTH FACT

Studies have shown that going for a short walk after a meal can improve your digestion. It also reduces the amount of sugar in your blood. This can help prevent Type 2 diabetes.

▲ It doesn't matter if you are active as part of a team or on your own. Any physical activity will have health benefits.

Being active doesn't have to mean going to a gym or running on a treadmill. Anything that gets you up and moving can help burn calories. Even walking to school or doing chores such as raking leaves will help. Joining a sports team is a great way to make friends while getting exercise. But there are also a lot of activities you can do on your own. Pick activities that you enjoy, and try to be active for at least 60 minutes every day.

▲ Riding your bike is a great way to get around town, parks, and country roads. It burns lots of calories too.

OTHER TREATMENT OPTIONS

For some people, eating less and exercising more aren't enough. A small number of people who are seriously overweight have surgery to help them lose weight. The operation doesn't remove the fat. Instead, it alters the digestive system. It makes the person feel full after meals that are smaller than he or she would normally eat.

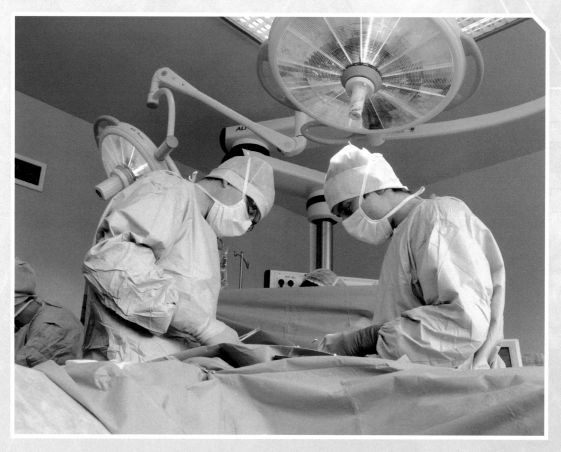

▲ Having an operation is a serious decision. A doctor will help advise a patient whether it is right for him or her.

In gastric band surgery, an inflatable balloon is placed around part of the stomach. Once this part of the stomach is full, the person will feel full. In gastric bypass surgery, a small pouch is made at the top of the stomach. This is the only part of the stomach that takes in food, which limits the amount a person can eat. Another type of surgery removes part of the stomach itself. Surgery can help people lose weight, but it is a last resort. It is not a magic cure for obesity. Patients still must watch their diet carefully and exercise. Surgery also has some health risks. For that reason, weight-loss surgery is only rarely performed on adolescents in their later teens.

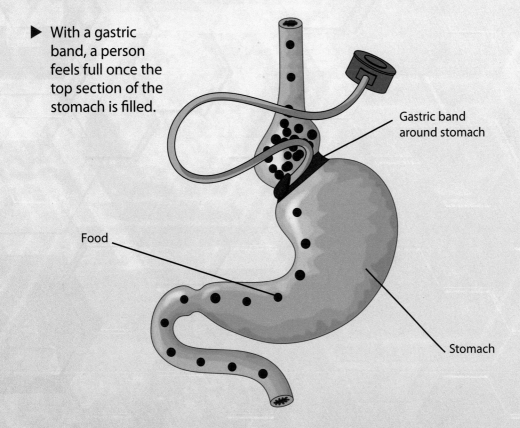

▶ With a gastric band, a person feels full once the top section of the stomach is filled.

Gastric band around stomach

Food

Stomach

CHAPTER 4
A HEALTHY LIFESTYLE

There are a lot of ideas about the best way to lose weight. If you go to a bookstore, you will find a whole shelf full of diet books. Each book promises results from a different diet plan. Your doctor can help you decide which one is best for you.

▶ Some diets replace meals with shakes. But they are no match for the nutrients found in fresh, natural foods.

HEALTH FACT

Scientists who study diets have discovered that people often do not benefit from a **crash diet**. They usually put the weight back on more quickly than people who have lost weight in a slower, healthier way.

Health Warning

There are many kinds of weight-loss or "diet" pills and supplements for sale. These promise to help people lose weight, but most don't work. They can also be very dangerous and can even lead to death. No one should ever take any medication that is not prescribed by the family doctor.

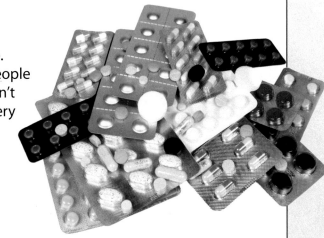

A lot of weight-loss diets promise quick results by restricting you to certain types of food. However, you need to eat a wide variety of foods to make sure that you're getting all the nutrients you need. Crash diets restrict you to a very small number of calories each day. They help some people lose weight in the short term, but they are not good for your body. Eating fresh, healthy food and exercising regularly are the best ways to a healthy lifestyle.

crash diet—a diet with the goal of losing weight quickly by eating very little

A NEW YOU

Some people who are obese focus on losing weight. Then, once they hit their target, they go back to their old habits. This often leads to them putting some of the weight they've lost right back on. Overcoming obesity means making lifestyle changes that continue even after you've reached a healthy weight.

▲ You should eat from fruit, vegetables, protein, grains, and dairy food groups daily. Try to vary your diet every day.

Your family's support for your healthy new lifestyle can really make a difference.

A healthy diet is something that will bring benefits for the rest of your life. Try for a good balance of different food groups, with a focus on fresh, natural ingredients. Learning how to cook your own food is fun. It will also help you be less dependent on unhealthy processed food or fast food. Get your whole family involved in eating healthy food and being active. Everyone will feel the benefits!

▶ Being active shouldn't stop once you've reached your target weight. Staying active will help keep you healthy.

KEEPING MOTIVATED

Most doctors recommend trying to lose 1 to 2 pounds (about 0.5 to 1 kg) per week. This means that getting down to a healthy weight can be a slow process. It's natural to feel discouraged sometimes. If you have a bad day and break your diet, don't feel sad about it. As long as you stick to your diet and exercise plan most of the time, you'll still make progress.

BREANNA'S STORY

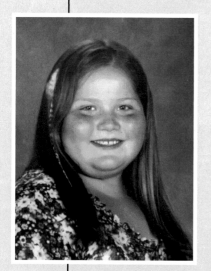

Breanna weighed 186 pounds (84 kg) when she was only 9 years old. She wanted to make a change. In just over a year, Breanna was able to get down to a healthy weight. She changed her diet and started exercising, including swimming and walking. Now Breanna competes in swimming and running competitions. She has even written a book about her weight-loss journey and has made a website too.

▶ Use experiences rather than food as a reward. Maybe you could go to a concert or watch your favorite team play a game.

Allowing yourself the occasional small treat will help you beat any cravings and stay on track. It is also important to keep focused on your goals. Do you have a target weight in mind? Or maybe you have a level of physical fitness that you want to achieve? Plan a reward for each step closer you get to your goal.

◀ Working toward a healthy weight can give you a great sense of achievement.

GLOSSARY

body fat (BAA-dee FAT)—tissue in the body that is made of up of cells that store fat. It is also called adipose tissue.

body mass index (BAA-dee MASS IN-dex)—a formula that compares height to weight to estimate how much body fat a person has. It is often shortened to BMI.

calorie (KA-luh-ree)—a unit used to measure the energy stored in food

carbohydrate (car-boh-HIE-drate)—a substance found in foods that provides energy for the body

crash diet (CRASH DIE-et)—a diet with the goal of losing weight quickly by eating very little

diabetes (die-uh-BEE-teez)—a disease in which the body cannot control the amount of sugar in the blood

digestive system (die-JES-tiv SIS-tum)—the body parts that work to break down food into substances that you can use

energy (EN-er-jee)—the ability to do work. Humans get their energy from food.

fat (FAT)—a substance found in foods that provides energy and does other important jobs in the body

gene (JEEN)—a code in a body's cells that tell it how to grow. Genes control characteristics such as hair color.

obesity (oh-BEE-si-tee)—the condition of being very overweight or fat

overweight (oh-ver-WAIT)—weighing more than is healthy for a person's age, height, and build

percentile (per-SEN-tile)—a value on a scale of 100 that shows the percentage that is equal to or below it

protein (PRO-teen)—a natural substance found in all living things that the body uses to build and repair itself

READ MORE

DK Publishing. *Human Body: A Visual Encyclopedia.* New York: Dorling Kindersley, 2012.

Hunt, Sara. *Stay Fit*: *Your Guide to Staying Active.* Mankato, Minn.: Capstone Press, 2012.

Lanser, Amanda. *School Lunches: Healthy Choices vs. Crowd Pleasers.* Mankato, Minn.: Compass Point Books, 2015.

Stewart, Sheila. *A Kid's Guide to Obesity.* Understanding Disease and Wellness. Vestal, N.Y.: Village Earth Press, 2013.

INTERNET SITES

FactHound offers a safe, fun way to find Internet sites related to this book. All of the sites on FactHound have been researched by our staff.

Here's all you do:

Visit *www.facthound.com*

Type in this code: 9781491482438

 Check out projects, games and lots more at
www.capstonekids.com

INDEX